Taking Care of Mango

A Story About Responsibility

Written by
Cindy Leaney

Illustrated by
Peter Wilks

Rourke
Publishing LLC
Vero Beach, Florida 32964

Before you read this story, take a look at the front cover of the book. Emily and Makayla are shown with a cat.

1. Who do you think is named Mango?

2. What do the girls seem to be doing?

3. How are they acting responsible?

Produced by SGA Illustration and Design
Designed by Phil Kay
Series Editor: Frank Sloan

www.rourkepublishing.com

Library of Congress Cataloging-in-0Publication Data

Leaney, Cindy.
    Taking care of Mango : responsibility / by Cindy Leaney ; illustrated by Peter Wilks.
        p. cm.-- (Hero club character)
    Summary: When their neighbor goes on a trip, Makayla and Emily care for her cat.
    ISBN 1-58952-738-0
    [1. Responsibility--Fiction. 2. Conduct of life--Fiction.] I. Title

PZ7.L46335Tak2003
    [E]--dc21

                                                        2003043231

Printed in the USA
MP/W

Welcome to The Hero Club!
Read about all the things that happen to them.
Try and guess what they'll do next.

www.theheroclub.com

4

"Could you take care of our cat,
Mango, while we're on vacation?"

"What's there to do?"

"She needs to be fed twice a day — morning and evening. She's going to have kittens in a few weeks."

"I wish I could help. Breakfast time is so busy trying to get everybody ready."

"We'll do it, Mom."

"Are you sure, Makayla?
This is a <u>big</u> responsibility."

"I can get up early on school mornings.
Emily can help me after school."

"Here's the key. Make sure you lock the door, and don't let anyone else in, please."

"Okay, Mrs. Ames. I'll be careful. I promise."

Everything was fine. Makayla got up 15 minutes early. She and Emily fed Mango and Mango purred.

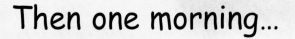

Then one morning...

"Oh no! Where's Mango?
Mango, Where are you?"

"Meow."

"Is Mango hurt?"

16

"We're taking care of my neighbor's cat. She had three kittens. They are <u>so</u> cute."

"Take us to see them."

"We can't. We made a promise."

"We'll ask them when they get back. Maybe they'll let you see the kittens."

"There aren't any kittens.
You just made them up."

"Thank you, Makayla. You and Emily did a great job."

"Some of the kids at school want to see the kittens. We said we would ask you."

"Okay. Bring them over on Saturday."

"Oh they're so cute. I wish I could have a kitten but our cat wouldn't like it."

"My mom says I'm too young."

"Would you like to choose a kitten, Makayla?"

"Yes, Makayla. Mrs. Ames already asked me. You proved you can take care of a pet."

"Thanks, Mom! Thanks, Mrs. Ames. Thanks, Mango."

WHAT DO YOU THINK?

Was it a good idea for Makayla and Emily to say that the other kids couldn't see the kittens until Mrs. Ames got back from vacation?

Why or why not?

IMPORTANT IDEAS

Responsibility—When something is your responsibility, it is your job or duty to make sure that it is done the way it is supposed to be.

On page 10, Makayla's mom says, "Are you sure, Makayla? This is a big responsibility."

What responsibilities do you have at home?

Now that you have read this book, see if you can answer these questions:

1. What things do Makayla and Emily agree to do in order to take care of Mango?

2. What extra things does Makayla's mother ask the girls to do?

3. Mango disappears. Where does the cat go and why?

About the author

Cindy Leaney teaches English and writes books for both young readers and adults. She has lived and worked in England, Kenya, Mexico, Saudi Arabia, and the United States.

About the illustrator

Peter Wilks began work in advertising, where he developed a love for illustration. He has drawn pictures for many children's books in Great Britain and in the United States.

HERO CLUB CHARACTER VALUE SERIES

Everyone Makes a Difference (A Book About Community)

Field Trip (A Book About Sharing)

It's Your Turn Now (A Book About Politeness)

Lost and Found (A Book About Honesty)

Summer Vacation (A Book About Patience)

Taking Care of Mango (A Book About Responsibility)